the
super,
epic,
mega
joke
book
for kids

the super, epic, mega joke book for kids

By Whee Whin

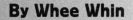

ZONDER**kidz**™

ZONDERKIDZ

The Super, Epic, Mega Joke Book for Kids
Copyright © 2016 by Zondervan

This title is also available as a Zondervan ebook.
Visit www.zondervan.com/ebooks

Requests for information should be addressed to:
Zonderkidz, 3900 *Sparks Dr. SE*, Grand Rapids, Michigan 49546

ISBN 978-0-310-75479-4

Cover design: Brand Navigation
Interior design: Denise Froehlich

Printed in the United States of America

17 18 19 20 21 22 23 24 /DCI/ 15 14 13 12 11 10 9 8 7 6 5 4 3

He will yet fill your mouth with laughter and
your lips with shouts of joy.

JOB 8:21

Table of Contents

Note to Jokesters

Jokes are a pretty common way for people to have some fun.

Lots of people tell them—kids and adults. Some are pretty funny. Some are very corny. Others make no sense at all. But no matter what your opinion of jokes is, one thing most people can agree on is that kids love them!! And I hope you are one of those kids because …

… if you are looking for a collection of funny, corny, crazy jokes this is the book for you!

The Super, Epic, Mega Joke Book for Kids is an awesome collection of good, clean, corny jokes that will make you roll your eyes, snort, giggles, groan, and laugh til you cry.

Knock, knock.
Who's there?
Hominy.
Hominy who?
Hominy jokes are you going to tell me today?

1

Knock-
Knock
Jokes

Knock, knock.
Who's there?
Fairy.
Fairy who?
Fairy pleased to meet you!

Knock, knock.
Who's there?
Atlas.
Atlas who?
Atlas it's Friday. No school tomorrow!

Knock, knock.
Who's there?
Boo.
Boo who?
Don't be sad!

Knock, knock.
Who's there?
Sara.
Sara who?
Sara 'nother way in?

Knock, knock.
Who's there?
Al.
Al who?
Al give you a hug if you let me in!

Knock, knock.
Who's there?
Simon.
Simon who?
Simon the other side of the door. If you opened up, you'd see!

Knock, knock.
Who's there?
Juno.
Juno who?
Juno who it is!

Knock, knock.
Who's there?
Guinea.
Guinea who?
Guinea high five!

Knock, knock.
Who's there?
Europe.
Europe who?
Europe to no good!

Knock, knock.
Who's there?
Sloane.
Sloane who?
Sloanely outside. Let me in!

Knock, knock.
Who's there?
Abbey.
Abbey who?
Abbey stung me on the nose!

Knock, knock.
Who's there?
Isaiah.
Isaiah who?
Isaiah 'gain—knock, knock!

Knock, knock.
Who's there?
Ohio.
Ohio who?
Oh, hi, how are you doing?

Knock, knock.
Who's there?
Sacha.
Sacha who?
Sacha lot of questions.

Knock, knock.
Who's there?
Babylon.
Babylon who?
Babylon. I'm not really listening anyway.

Knock, knock.
Who's there?
Dwayne.
Dwayne who?
Dwayne the bathtub, it's overflowing!

Knock, knock.
Who's there?
Avenue.
Avenue who?
Avenue heard this joke before?

Knock, knock.
Who's there?
Emma.
Emma who?
Emma bit cold out here, could you let me in?

Knock, knock.
Who's there?
Maya.
Maya who?
Maya name is Dan.

Knock, knock.
Who's there?
Area.
Area who?
Area there? It's me!

Knock, knock.
Who's there?
Lena.
Lena who?
Lena little closer and I'll tell you.

Knock, knock.
Who's there?
Jamaica.
Jamaica who?
Jamaica great friend!

Knock, knock.
Who's there?
Justin.
Justin who?
Justin the neighborhood. Thought I would drop by.

Knock, knock.
Who's there?
Chile.
Chile who?
It's getting Chile out here, let me in!

Knock, knock.
Who's there?
Noah.
Noah who?
Noah good place we can get something to eat?

Knock, knock.
Who's there?
Heaven.
Heaven who?
Heaven seen you in a while.

Knock, knock.
Who's there?
Brad.
Brad who?
I've got Brad news, I'm afraid!

Knock, knock.
Who's there?
Germany.
Germany who?
Germany people knock on your door?

Knock, knock.
Who's there?
Aisle.
Aisle who?
Aisle see you around!

Knock, knock.
Who's there?
Stan.
Stan who?
Stan back! I'm knocking this door down!

Knock, knock.
Who's there?
Juneau.
Juneau who?
Juneau what time it is?

Knock, knock.
Who's there?
Owen.
Owen who?
Owen are you going to let me in?

Knock, knock.
Who's there?
Adore.
Adore who?
Adore is between us. Open up!

Knock, knock.
Who's there?
Osborn.
Osborn who?
Osborn today—it's my birthday!

Knock, knock.
Who's there?
Abby.
Abby who?
Abby birthday to you!

Knock, knock.
Who's there?
Wanda.
Wanda who?
Wanda wish you a happy birthday!

Knock, knock.
Who's there?
William.
William who?
William, mind your own business?

Knock, knock.
Who's there?
Snow.
Snow who?
Snow use, I forgot my name!

Knock, knock.
Who's there?
Justin.
Justin who?
Justin time for dinner!

Knock, knock.
Who's there?
Honeydew.
Honeydew who?
Honeydew you want to hear a knock-knock joke?

Knock, knock.
Who's there?
Cain.
Cain who?
Cain I come in, please?

Knock, knock.
Who's there?
Orange.
Orange who?
Orange you going to let me in?

Knock, knock.
Who's there?
Linda.
Linda who?
Linda hand! I can't do it all by myself!

Knock, knock.
Who's there?
Dora.
Dora who?
Dora's locked. That's why I'm knocking!

Knock, knock.
Who's there?
Doughnut.
Doughnut who?
Doughnut ask, it's a secret!

Knock, knock.
Who's there?
Annie.
Annie who?
Annie body home?

Knock, knock.
Who's there?
Lettuce.
Lettuce who?
Lettuce in, it's cold out here!

Knock, knock.
Who's there?
Mikey.
Mikey who?
Mikey doesn't fit in the hole!

Knock, knock.
Who's there?
Beets.
Beets who?
Beets me!

Knock, knock.
Who's there?
Kiwi.
Kiwi who?
Kiwi go to the store?

Knock, knock.
Who's there?
Cash.
Cash who?
I knew you were a nut!

Knock, knock.
Who's there?
Kent.
Kent who?
Kent you tell by my voice?

Knock, knock.
Who's there?
Theodore.
Theodore who?
Theodore was locked so I knocked!

Knock, knock.
Who's there?
Ice cream.
Ice cream who?
Ice cream if you don't let me in!

Knock, knock.
Who's there?
Turnip.
Turnip who?
Turnip the volume, it's too quiet.

Knock, knock.
Who's there?
Luke.
Luke who?
Luke through the peephole and find out!

Knock, knock.
Who's there?
Ketchup.
Ketchup who?
Ketchup with you soon!

Knock, knock.
Who's there?
Abbott.
Abbott who?
Abbott time you opened this door!

Knock, knock.
Who's there?
Beef.
Beef who?
Beef-or I get cold, you'd better let me in!

Knock, knock.
Who's there?
Jess.
Jess who?
Jess open the door and stop asking questions!

Knock, knock.
Who's there?
Cook.
Cook who?
Hey! Who you calling cuckoo?

Knock, knock.
Who's there?
Barry.
Barry who?
Barry nice to see you!

Knock, knock.
Who's there?
Bean.
Bean who?
Bean fishing lately?

Knock, knock.
Who's there?
Figs.
Figs who?
Figs the doorbell, it's broken!

Knock, knock.
Who's there?
Aida.
Aida who?
Aida sandwich for lunch today. Do you want one?

Knock, knock.
Who's there?
Bean.
Bean who?
Bean a while since I saw you last!

Knock, knock.
Who's there?
Pete.
Pete who?
Pete-za delivery!

Knock, knock.
Who's there?
Broccoli.
Broccoli who?
Broccoli doesn't have a last name, silly!

Knock, knock.
Who's there?
Howard.
Howard who?
Howard you?

Knock, knock.
Who's there?
Water.
Water who?
Water way to answer the door!

Knock, knock.
Who's there?
Omelet.
Omelet who?
Omelet smarter than I look.

Knock, knock.
Who's there?
You be.
You be who?
You be a pal and bring me a cookie!

Knock, knock.
Who's there?
Orange juice.
Orange juice who?
Orange juice going to invite me in?

Knock, knock.
Who's there?
Anita.
Anita who?
Anita borrow a pencil.

Knock, knock.
Who's there?
Butter.
Butter who?
It's butter if you don't know!

Knock, knock.
Who's there?
Doughnut.
Doughnut who?
Doughnut be afraid, it's just me!

Knock, knock.
Who's there?
Arfur.
Arfur who?
Arfur got!

Knock, knock.
Who's there?
Denise.
Denise who?
Denise are above the ankles.

Knock, knock.
Who's there?
Peas.
Peas who?
Peas open the door for me!

Knock, knock.
Who's there?
Water.
Water who?
Water you doing?

Knock, knock.
Who's there?
Phillip.
Phillip who?
Phillip your pool. I wanna take a dip!

Knock, knock.
Who's there?
Jo.
Jo who?
Jo King!

Knock, knock.
Who's there?
Danielle.
Danielle who?
Danielle so loud! I heard you the first time!

Knock, knock.
Who's there?
Banana.
Banana who?
Knock, knock.
Who's there?
Banana.
Banana who?
Knock, knock.
Who's there?
Orange.
Orange who?
Orange you glad I didn't say banana?

Knock, knock.
Who's there?
Cereal.
Cereal who?
Cereal pleasure to meet you!

Knock, knock
Who's there?
Radio.
Radio who?
Radio not, here I come!

Knock, knock.
Who's there?
Canoe.
Canoe who?
Canoe come over and play?

Knock, knock.
Who's there?
Rita.
Rita who?
Rita book, you might learn something!

Knock, knock.
Who's there?
Dishes.
Dishes who?
Dishes me, who are you?

Knock, knock.
Who's there?
Cargo.
Cargo who?
Cargo "beep, beep, vroom, vroom!"

Knock, knock.
Who's there?
Wooden shoe.
Wooden shoe who?
Wooden shoe like to know?

Knock, knock.
Who's there?
Isabel.
Isabel who?
Isabel working? I had to knock!

Knock, knock.
Who's there?
Isaiah.
Isaiah who?
Isaiah nothing until you open this door!

Knock, knock.
Who's there?
Max.
Max who?
Max no difference!

Knock, knock.
Who's there?
Juicy.
Juicy who?
Juicy my set of keys?

Knock, knock.
Who's there?
Needle.
Needle who?
Needle little money for the movies!

Knock, knock.
Who's there?
Iva.
Iva who?
Iva sore hand from knocking.

Knock, knock.
Who's there?
One shoe.
One shoe who?
One shoe play with me?

Knock, knock.
Who's there?
A broken pencil.
A broken pencil who?
Never mind. It's pointless!

Knock, knock.
Who's there?
Ali.
Ali who?
Ali wanna do is have some fun.

Knock, knock.
Who's there?
Barbie.
Barbie who?
Barbie Q. Chicken!

Knock, knock.
Who's there?
Dishes.
Dishes who?
Dishes the FBI, open up!

Knock, knock.
Who's there?
Nana.
Nana who?
Nana your business!

Knock, knock.
Who's there?
Fiddle.
Fiddle who?
Fiddle make you happy, I'll tell you!

Knock, knock.
Who's there?
Stopwatch.
Stopwatch who?
Stopwatch you're doing right this minute!

Knock, knock.
Who's there?
Ivan.
Ivan who?
Ivan idea you know who it is!

Knock, knock.
Who's there?
Razor.
Razor who?
Razor hands in the air like you just don't care!

Knock, knock.
Who's there?
Althea.
Althea who?
Althea later alligator!

Knock, knock.
Who's there?
Train.
Train who?
Someone needs to train ya' to open the door!

Knock, knock.
Who's there?
Uriah.
Uriah who?
Keep uriah on the ball!

Knock, knock.
Who's there?
Dishes.
Dishes who?
Dishes a nice place!

Knock, knock.
Who's there?
Wooden shoe.
Wooden shoe who?
Wooden shoe like to hear another joke?

Knock, knock.
Who's there?
Knock.
Knock who?
Knock, knock!
Who's there?
Knock.
Knock who?
Knock, knock!
Who's there?
Knock.
Knock who?
Knock, knock!
Who's there?
Knock.
Knock who?
Knock, knock!
. . . . Ok, well come on in then.

Knock, knock.
Who's there?
Yah!
Yah who?
Did I just hear a cowboy in there?

Knock, knock.
Who's there?
Amy.
Amy who?
Amy 'fraid I've forgotten.

Knock, knock.
Who's there?
Mustache.
Mustache who?
Please let me in. I mustache you a question!

Knock, knock.
Who's there?
Meg.
Meg who?
Meg up your mind! Are you going to let me in or not?

Knock, knock.
Who's there?
Weevil.
Weevil who?
Weevil only be staying a minute.

Knock, knock.
Who's there?
Hal.
Hal who?
Hal-loo to you too!

Knock, knock.
Who's there?
Ben.
Ben who?
Ben knocking for ten minutes!

Knock, knock.
Who's there?
Says.
Says who?
Says me, that's who!

Knock, knock.
Who's there?
Harry.
Harry who?
Harry up, it's cold out here!

Knock, knock.
Who's there?
Ear.
Ear who?
Ear you are! I've been looking for you!

Knock, knock.
Who's there?
Sing.
Sing who?
Whooooooo!

Knock, knock.
Who's there?
Mia.
Mia who?
Mia and my shadow!

Knock, knock.
It's open!

Knock, knock.
Who's there?
Bingo.
Bingo who?
Bingo'ng to come see you for ages.

Knock, knock.
Who's there?
Shelby.
Shelby who?
Shelby coming around the mountain when she comes.
Shelby coming around the mountain when she comes.
Shelby coming around the mountain.
Shelby coming around the mountain.
Shelby coming around the mountain when she comes!

Knock, knock.
Who's there?
Ammonia.
Ammonia who?
Ammonia little kid!

Knock, knock.
Who's there?
I am.
I am who?
You mean you don't remember who you are?

Knock, knock.
Who's there?
Ears.
Ears who?
Ears some more knock-knock jokes for you!

Knock, knock.
Who's there?
Bless.
Bless who?
I didn't sneeze!

Knock, knock.
Who's there?
Dots.
Dots who?
Dots for me to know and you to find out!

Knock, knock.
Who's there?
Winner.
Winner who?
Winner you going to let me in?

Knock, knock.
Who's there?
Maura.
Maura who?
Maura the merrier!

Knock, knock.
Who's there?
Dewey.
Dewey who?
Dewey have to keep telling silly jokes?

Knock, knock.
Who's there?
Dawn.
Dawn who?
Dawn leave me out in the cold!

Knock, knock.
Who's there?
Scold.
Scold who?
Scold outside!

Knock, knock.
Who's there?
Mary Lee.
Mary Lee who?
Mary Lee, Mary Lee, Mary Lee, Mary Lee, life is but a dream!

Knock, knock.
Who's there?
Hebrews.
Hebrews who?
Hebrews some good coffee.

Knock, knock.
Who's there?
You don't remember me?

Knock, knock.
Who's there?
You know.
You know who?
Ah. It's You-know-who!

Knock, knock.
Who's there?
Abe.
Abe who?
Abe C D E F G . . .

Knock, knock.
Who's there?
Leaf.
Leaf who?
Leaf me alone!

Knock, knock.
Who's there?
Diploma.
Diploma who?
Diploma is here to fix the sink.

Knock, knock.
Who's there?
Omar.
Omar who?
Omar goodness! This is the wrong door!

Knock, knock.
Who's there?
Repeat.
Repeat who?
Who, who, who, who, who. How long do I have to do this?

Knock, knock.
Who's there?
Hoover.
Hoover who?
Hoover you expecting?

Knock, knock.
Who's there?
Greta.
Greta who?
You Greta on my nerves!

Knock, knock.
Who's there?
Yukon.
Yukon who?
Yukon say that again!

Knock, knock.
Who's there?
Nobel.
Nobel who?
No bell, that's why I knocked!

Knock, knock.
Who's there?
Disguise.
Disguise who?
Disguise your best friend?

Knock, knock.
Who's there?
Alex.
Alex who?
Alex-plain later!

Knock, knock.
Who's there?
Usher.
Usher who?
Usher wish you would let me in!

Knock, knock.
Who's there?
Alma.
Alma who?
Alma not going to tell you.

Knock, knock.
Who's there?
Churchill.
Churchill who?
Churchill be held on Sunday!

Knock, knock.
Who's there?
Noise.
Noise who?
Noise to see you! How have you been?

Knock, knock.
Who's there?
Icon.
Icon who?
Icon tell you another knock-knock joke if you want!

Knock, knock.
Who's there?
Freeze.
Freeze who?
Freeze a jolly good fellow!
Freeze a jolly good fellow!
Freeze a jolly good fellow!
Which nobody can deny!

Knock, knock.
Who's there?
Passion.
Passion who?
Passion through and thought I'd come say hello!

Knock, knock.
Who's there?
Argue.
Argue who?
Argue going to let me in?

Knock, knock.
Who's there?
Gladys.
Gladys who?
Gladys the weekend, aren't you?

Knock, knock.
Who's there?
Bashful.
Bashful who?
I can't say, I'm too embarrassed!

Knock, knock.
Who's there?
Ivana.
Ivana who?
Ivana come in!

Knock, knock.
Who's there?
Woo.
Woo who?
Don't get so excited, it's just a joke!

Knock, knock.
Who's there?
Howard.
Howard who?
Howard can it be to guess a knock-knock joke?

Knock, knock.
Who's there?
Knee.
Knee who?
Knee-d you ask?

Knock, knock.
Who's there?
Mischa.
Mischa who?
I Mischa a lot!

Knock, knock.
Who's there?
Dozen.
Dozen who?
Dozen anybody want to let me in?

Knock, knock.
Who's there?
A little old lady.
A little old lady who?
I didn't know you could yodel!

Knock, knock.
Who's there?
Carl.
Carl who?
Carl get you there faster than a bike!

Knock, knock.
Who's there?
Avery.
Avery who?
Avery time I come to your house we go through this again!

Knock, knock.
Who's there?
Hatch.
Hatch who?
God bless you!

Knock, knock.
Who's there?
Hacienda.
Hacienda who?
Hacienda the joke!

Knock, knock.
Who's there?
Norma Lee.
Norma Lee who?
Norma Lee I don't go around knocking on doors, but I just had to meet you!

Knock, knock.
Who's there?
Issue.
Issue who?
Issue blind? It's me!

Knock, knock.
Who's there?
Tank.
Tank who?
You're welcome!

Knock, knock.
Who's there?
Ratio.
Ratio who?
Ratio to the end of the street!

Knock, knock.
Who's there?
Les.
Les who?
Les go out and play.

Knock, knock.
Who's there?
Hominy.
Hominy who?
Hominy times are we going to have to go through this?

Knock, knock.
Who's there?
Police.
Police who?
Police hurry up, it's chilly outside!

Knock, knock.
Who's there?
Knock, knock.
Who's there?
You're supposed to say "knock, knock who!"

Knock, knock.
Who's there?
Impatient pirate.
Impatient p—
ARRRRRRRRRR!

Knock, knock.
Who's there?
Opportunity.
Opportunity who?
Opportunity doesn't knock twice!

Knock, knock.
Who's there?
Zany.
Zany who?
Zany body home?

Knock, knock.
Who's there?
Waddle.
Waddle who?
Waddle you give me if I go away?

Knock, knock.
Who's there?
Haman.
Haman who?
Haman! It's cold out here!

Knock, knock.
Who's there?
Handsome.
Handsome who?
Handsome money through the keyhole and I'll tell you!

Knock, knock.
Who's there?
Champ.
Champ who?
Champ poo your hair—it's dirty!

Knock, knock.
Who's there?
Oswald.
Oswald who?
Oswald my bubblegum.

Knock, knock.
Who's there?
Tiss.
Tiss who?
Tiss who is good for blowing your nose!

Knock, knock.
Who's there?
Sam.
Sam who?
Sam day you'll recognize me.

Knock, knock.
Who's there?
Adam.
Adam who?
Adam my way, I'm coming through!

Knock, knock.
Who's there?
Spell.
Spell who?
W-H-O

Knock, knock.
Who's there?
Yah.
Yah who?
Wow. You sure are excited to see me!

Knock, knock.
Who's there?
A little boy.
A little boy who?
A little boy who can't reach the doorbell!

Knock, knock.
Who's there?
Ida.
Ida who?
Ida know. Sorry!

Knock, knock.
Who's there?
Voodoo.
Voodoo who?
Voodoo you think you are?

Knock, knock.
Who's there?
Mae.
Mae who?
Mae be I'll tell you and maybe I won't!

Knock, knock.
Who's there?
Doorbell repairman!
Doorbell repairman who?
Ding dong! My work here is done.

Knock, knock.
Who's there?
Colleen.
Colleen who?
Colleen yourself up. You're a mess!

Knock, knock.
Who's there?
Tuba.
Tuba who?
Tuba two they went marching into Noah's ark.

Knock, knock.
Who's there?
Marie.
Marie who?
Marie me? I love you!

Knock, knock.
Who's there?
G.I.
G.I. who?
G.I. really don't know.

Knock, knock.
Who's there?
Kenya.
Kenya who?
Kenya keep the noise down? I'm trying to sleep!

Knock, knock.
Who's there?
Gus.
Gus who?
That's what you're supposed to do!

Knock, knock.
Who's there?
Koala.
Koala who?
Koala the cops. I've been robbed!

Knock, knock.
Who's there?
Howdy.
Howdy who?
Not howdy who, howdy do.

Knock, knock.
Who's there?
Olive.
Olive who?
Olive right next door.

Knock, knock.
Who's there?
Luke.
Luke who?
Luke through the peephole and find out.

Knock, knock.
Who's there?
Cat.
Cat who?
Cat you think of a better joke than that?

Knock, knock.
Who's there?
Heart.
Heart who?
Heart you glad to see me?

Knock, knock.
Who's there?
Uruguay.
Uruguay who?
You go Uruguay and I'll go mine!

Knock, knock.
Who's there?
Sawyer.
Sawyer who?
Sawyer the one who likes knock-knock jokes.

Knock, knock.
Who's there?
Sarah.
Sarah who?
Sarah doorbell around here somewhere?

Knock, knock.
Who's there?
Pudding.
Pudding who?
Just pudding the final touches on painting your door.

Knock, knock.
Who's there?
Olive.
Olive who?
Olive to serve.

Knock, knock.
Who's there?
Shirley.
Shirley who?
Shirley you must know me by now!

Knock, knock.
Who's there?
Gum.
Gum who?
Gum on, let me in already!

Knock, knock.
Who's there?
Olive.
Olive who?
Olive near your cousin.

Knock, knock.
Who's there?
Norway.
Norway who?
Norway will I leave until you open this door!

Knock, knock.
Who's there?
Manuel.
Manuel who?
Manuel be sorry if you don't answer this door!

Knock, knock.
Who's there?
You.
You who?
Are you trying to get my attention?

Knock, knock.
Who's there?
Goliath.
Goliath who?
Goliath down, you looketh tired.

Knock, knock.
Who's there?
Iran.
Iran who?
Iran all the way over here to tell you something.

Knock, knock.
Who's there?
Fairy.
Fairy who?
Fairy pleased to meet you!

Knock, knock.
Who's there?
Alison.
Alison, who?
Alison to you if you listen to me!

Knock, knock.
Who's there?
Ken.
Ken who?
Ken you open the door and let me in?

Knock, knock.
Who's there?
Howl.
Howl who?
Howl you know unless you open the door?

Knock, knock.
Who's there?
Scott.
Scott who?
Scott nothing to do with you!

Knock, knock.
Who's there?
Cash.
Cash who?
No thanks, I prefer peanuts.

Knock, knock.
Who's there?
Indonesia.
Indonesia who?
I see you and I get weak Indonesia!

Knock, knock.
Who's there?
Jell-O.
Jell-O who?
Jell-O, it's me again.

Knock, knock.
Who's there?
Elias.
Oh, hi, Elias, come in, come in.
You're supposed to say, "Elias who?"

Knock, knock.
Who's there?
Hawaii.
Hawaii who?
Hawaii doing?

Knock, knock.
Who's there?
Ewan.
Ewan who?
No, it's just me!

Knock, knock.
Who's there?
Ice-cream soda.
Ice-cream soda who?
Ice-cream soda whole world will know how silly I am.

Knock, knock.
Who's there?
Wanda.
Wanda who?
Wanda buy some Girl Scout cookies?

Knock, knock.
Who's there?
Avocado.
Avocado who?
Avocado cold. Ah-choo!

Knock, knock.
Who's there?
Nadia.
Nadia who?
Nadia head if you understand me.

Knock, knock.
Who's there?
Alaska.
Alaska who?
Alaska 'nother person if you don't know the answer.

Knock, knock.
Who's there?
Hair.
Hair who?
Hair you are!

Knock, knock.
Who's there?
Doris.
Doris who?
Doris locked, that's why I knocked!

Knock, knock.
Who's there?
Butternut.
Butternut who?
Butternut let me in—my feet are muddy.

Knock, knock.
Who's there?
Sarah.
Sara who?
Sarah phone I could use?

Knock, knock.
Who's there?
Sabina.
Sabina who?
Sabina long time since I've seen you!

Knock, knock.
Who's there?
Isolate.
Isolate who?
Isolate to the party, I almost missed it.

Knock, knock.
Who's there?
Olive.
Olive who?
Olive you so much.

Knock, knock.
Who's there?
Phyllis.
Phyllis who?
Phyllis cup up with water, please. I'm thirsty!

Knock, knock.
Who's there?
Rufus.
Rufus who?
Rufus covered in snow. Let me in before it slides off!

Knock, knock.
Who's there?
Juan.
Juan who?
Juan to hear some more of these knock-knock jokes?

Knock, knock.
Who's there?
Russian.
Russian who?
Stop Russian me!

Knock, knock.
Who's there?
Ida.
Ida who?
Ida like to be your friend!

Knock, knock.
Who's there?
Benny.
Benny who?
Benny thing happening with you today?

Knock, knock.
Who's there?
Lime.
Lime who?
Lime leaving if you don't open the door!

Knock, knock.
Who's there?
Wah.
Wah who?
Why are you so happy?

Knock, knock.
Who's there?
Wood.
Wood who?
Wood you laugh at my jokes?

Knock, knock.
Who's there?
Howard.
Howard who?
Howard you know unless you open the door?

Knock, knock.
Who's there?
Frank.
Frank who?
Frank you for being my friend.

Knock, knock.
Who's there?
Utah.
Utah who?
Utah-king to me?

Knock, knock.
Who's there?
Venice.
Venice who?
Venice your mother coming home?

2

Question and Answer Jokes

Why was the letter so wet?
There was postage dew.

What do you call an angry Teddy bear?
Furry-ous.

What does a pirate say on his 80th birthday?
Aye m-atey.

Why was the broom late for school?
It swept too late.

What is it called when a scientist spits out her gum?
An ex-spearmint.

Which road does a tree take?
Root 66.

Where does Tarzan work out?
A jungle gym.

What kind of music do planets listen to?
Neptunes.

**Where does pizza go when
it commits a crime?**
The food court.

What does a cat say when it sees a mouse?
Meow-se.

**What does a mommy squirrel say
when her baby has been naughty?**
You're nuttin' but trouble.

Which is the richest fish?
A goldfish.

What has a neck but no head?
A bottle.

Which knight wrote at the round table?
King Author.

Where do computers grow?
On Apple trees.

Why is it really hot in a stadium after a football game?
All the fans have left.

What did the big bucket say to the little bucket?
You look a little pail.

Why did the cookie go to the hospital?
He was feeling crumby.

What has four legs but can't walk?
A chair.

How do you make an egg roll?
Push it.

**Why did the lady want wheels
on her rocking chair?**
So she could rock and roll.

**What did the hot dog say
when it won the race?**
I'm the wiener.

**Who can shave six times a day,
but still have a beard?**
A barber.

Why were the ink spots crying?
Because their mother was in the pen.

**What do you get when you
stack a bunch of pizzas?**
The Leaning Tower of Pizza.

Did you hear about the kid who drank 8 lemonades?
He burped 7 up.

What kind of crackers do firemen like in their soup?
Firecrackers.

Why did the grape stop in the middle of the road?
Because he ran out of juice.

What did the egg say to the person?
You crack me up.

What do you get if you eat beans and onions?
Tear gas.

What is brown and sticky?
A stick.

**Why shouldn't you play hide
and seek with a mountain?**
Because it always peeks.

When is a vet the busiest?
When it is raining cats and dogs.

Who stole the soap from the bathtub?
The robber duckie.

**What do you call a potato
that watches football?**
A spec-tator.

**What do you call a wheel
that gives speeches?**
A spokesman.

**What do churches and mountains
have in common?**
They both have steep steeples.

Which baseball player holds the lemonade?
The pitcher.

When is fishing not relaxing?
When you are the worm.

Why can't you tell jokes on the ice?
It will crack up.

Who is the shortest person in the Bible?
Nehemiah.

Why did the policeman stay in bed?
He was under cover.

Why did the little girl's tooth fall out?
Because it was looth.

What did one eye say to the other?
Between you and me, something smells.

Why was 6 afraid of 7?
Because 7 8 9.

**Why can't you explain puns
to kleptomaniacs?**
They always take things, literally.

Why did the computer crash?
It had a bad driver.

What do you call a happy cowboy?
A jolly rancher.

What's the best thing to put into pie?
Your teeth.

**What do you get when you cross
a piece of paper and scissors?**
Confetti.

Why shouldn't you tell an egg a joke?
It might crack up.

When do astronauts eat?
At launch time.

What is a cheerleader's favorite color?
Yeller.

**What did one volcano say
to the other volcano?**
I lava you.

**Why didn't the quarter roll down
the hill with the nickel?**
Because it had more cents.

**What kind of lighting did
Noah use on the ark?**
Floodlights.

**Why were the early days of
history called the dark ages?**
Because there were so many knights.

Why did the teacher wear sunglasses?
Because his class was so bright.

Why were the teacher's eyes crossed?
She couldn't control her pupils.

**Why did the policeman go
to the baseball game?**
He heard someone had stolen a base.

What do lawyers wear to court?
Lawsuits.

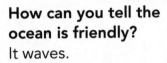

**How can you tell the
ocean is friendly?**
It waves.

What's a tornado's favorite game?
Twister.

**What did the ground say
to the earthquake?**
You crack me up.

**What kind of tree can
fit in your hand?**
A palm tree.

What makes music on your head?
A head band.

What did the windmill say when she met her favorite movie star?
Nice to meet you. I'm a BIG FAN.

What did the big chimney say to the small chimney?
You're too young to smoke.

Why did the belt go to jail?
He held up a pair of pants.

Why was the cook frustrated?
He was running out of thyme.

What did the blanket say to the bed?
Don't worry, I've got you covered.

Why did the house go to the doctor?
It had window panes.

What has four wheels and flies?
A garbage truck.

What is easy to get into but hard to get out of?
Trouble.

Why did the poor man sell yeast?
To make some dough.

What did the football coach say to the vending machine?
Give me my quarterback.

Did you hear about the guy who lost his whole left side?
He's all right now.

What did the baby corn say to the mama corn?
Where's popcorn?

Where does the president keep his armies?
In his sleevies.

How did the barber win the race?
He knew a short cut.

Why was the man running around his bed?
He wanted to catch up on his sleep.

How did the farmer fix his jeans?
With a cabbage patch.

What do you call cheese that's not yours?
Nacho cheese.

Where do pencils go on vacation?
Pencil-vania.

Why did the boy bring a ladder to school?
He wanted to go to high school.

Why did the girl spread peanut butter on the road?
To go with the traffic jam.

What do you call a loony spaceman?
An astro-nut.

What do clouds wear under their shorts?
Thunderpants.

What did the paper say to the pencil?
Write on.

Why do bananas put sunscreen on before they go in the sun?
They might peel.

Did you hear about the fire at the circus?
It was in tents.

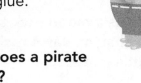

How do you fix a tuba?
With a tuba glue.

**How much does a pirate
pay for corn?**
A buccaneer.

Why did the sun go to school?
To get brighter.

What is the ocean's favorite subject?
Current events.

**Why shouldn't you write
with a broken pencil?**
Because it's pointless.

What did the policeman say to his tummy?
You're under a vest.

Why does a moon rock taste better than an earth rock?
It's a little meteor.

Why did the cabbage win the race?
Because it was ahead.

What do calendars eat?
Dates.

Why did Cinderella get kicked off the softball team?
Because she ran away from the ball.

What goes up and down but does not move?
Stairs.

Where should a 500-pound alien go?
On a diet.

What did one toilet say to the other?
You look a bit flushed.

Why did the picture go to jail?
Because it was framed.

What did one wall say to the other wall?
I'll meet you at the corner.

What washes up on tiny beaches?
Microwaves.

Why did the opera singer go sailing?
She wanted to hit the high C's.

What is a boxer's favorite drink?
Punch.

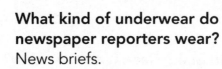

What kind of underwear do newspaper reporters wear?
News briefs.

What did Tennessee?
The same thing Arkansas.

How do you make a fire with two sticks?
Make sure one is a match.

What did one penny say to the other penny?
We make cents together.

How do you cut a wave in half?
Use a sea saw.

Why was the boy sitting on his watch?
Because he wanted to be on time.

Why does the Mississippi River see so well?
It has four eyes.

What did one hat say to the other?
Stay here, I'll go on ahead.

What kind of music do planets sing?
Neptunes.

Where would an astronaut park his space ship?
A parking meteor.

What is a tree's favorite drink?
Root beer.

Why did the cantaloupe jump in the lake?
Because it wanted to be a watermelon.

What gets wetter the more it dries?
A towel.

What kind of nails do carpenters hate hammering?
Fingernails.

Why was the broom late?
It over-swept.

What do you call a banana that has been cut in half?
A banana split.

Why did the golfer wear two pairs of pants?
In case he got a hole in one.

Why did the reporter walk into the ice cream shop?
Because he wanted a scoop.

What is the tallest building in any city?
A library, it has many stories.

Why did the student eat his homework?
The teacher told him it was a piece of cake.

Why was Cinderella so bad at sports?
Because she had a pumpkin for a coach.

Why did the farmer cross the road?
To catch the chicken.

Where does seaweed look for a job?
In the kelp wanted ads.

What's the slipperiest country?
Greece.

What is the fiercest flower in the garden?
The tiger lily.

**What do postal workers do
when they're angry?**
They stamp their feet.

How can you tell a train just went by?
It left its tracks.

**What did the laundryman say to
the impatient customer?**
"Keep your shirt on."

What kind of flower is on your face?
Tulips.

**Why are the floors of basketball
courts always so damp?**
The players dribble.

**What is it that even the most
careful person overlooks?**
Her nose.

Why do bicycles fall over?
Because they are two-tired.

What's a golfer's favorite letter?
T.

Why was everyone so tired on April 1st?
They had just finished a March of 31 days.

Why did the cookie cry?
Because his mom was a wafer so long.

What is the world's longest punctuation mark?
The hundred yard dash.

**What starts with E, ends with E
and only has one letter?**
An envelope.

Why are traffic lights never ready on time?
Because they take too long to change.

What did Mars say to Saturn?
Give me a ring sometime.

How do trains hear?
Through their engineers.

Why did the basketball player go to jail?
Because he shot the ball.

What is black, white, green, and bumpy?
A pickle wearing a tuxedo.

What did the ceiling say to the chandelier?
You're the bright spot in my life.

**Why did the robber take a bath
before he stole from the bank?**
He wanted to make a clean get away.

**What two things can you not
have for breakfast?**
Lunch and dinner.

Why did the tree go to the dentist?
It needed a root canal.

What new crop did the farmer plant?
Beets me.

What do you call an underwater spy?
James Pond.

**What do you get when you cross
a computer and a life guard?**
A screensaver.

Why did the orange lose the race?
Because he ran out of juice.

**What kind of plates do
they use on Venus?**
Flying saucers.

What did Delaware?
A New Jersey.

**Have you heard the rumor
about the butter?**
I better not tell you, it might spread.

**What kind of match can't
be set on fire?**
A tennis match.

What does a piece of toast wear to bed?
His pa-JAM-as.

**What do you call a boomerang
that does not come back?**
A stick!

**What do you get when you cross a
football player with a pay phone?**
A wide receiver.

**What do you get when you cross a
hamburger with a computer?**
A big mac!

What kind of bagel can fly?
A plain bagel.

**Who did the pharaoh talk
to when he was sad?**
His mummy.

How do barbers speed up their jobs?
They make short cuts.

Why was the math book upset?
It had a lot of problems.

Where do cars get the most flat tires?
At forks in the road.

**How many books can you put
into an empty backpack?**
One—after that it isn't empty.

How many months have 28 days?
All of them.

How many letters are in The Alphabet?
There are 11 letters in The Alphabet.

Waiter, will my pizza be long?
No sir, it will be round.

Which weighs more, a ton of feathers or a ton of bricks?
Neither—they both weigh a ton.

What has a head and tail, is brown, and has no legs?
A penny.

What do you call candy that's been stolen?
Hot chocolate.

How do you make a walnut laugh?
Crack it up.

How do you make a milk shake?
Give it a good scare.

What is a pretzel's favorite dance?
The twist.

What kind of band can't play music?
A rubber band.

What do hockey players and magicians have in common?
Both do hat tricks.

Why was there thunder and lightning in the lab?
The scientists were brainstorming.

Why was the nose tired?
Because it had been running all day.

Why are some pirates mean?
Because they just RRRRRR.

What did the hamburger give his sweetheart?
An onion ring.

Why doesn't anyone want to be friends with a clock?
All it does is tock-tock-tock.

What kind of apple has a short temper?
A crab apple.

Why do bankers eat by themselves?
They're loaners.

When does it rain money?
When there is change in the weather.

What did the fork say to the knife?
You're looking sharp.

Where did the computer go to dance?
To a disc-o.

What are the strongest days of the week?
Saturday and Sunday. Every other day is a weekday.

Did you hear the joke about the roof?
Never mind, it's over your head.

Why did the Oreo go to the dentist?
Because he lost his filling.

What do you call a funny mountain?
Hill-arious.

Why can't your nose be 12 inches long?
Because then it would be a foot.

What kind of button won't unbutton?
A belly button.

Where do crayons go on vacation?
Color-ado.

What kind of a teacher passes gas?
A tutor.

What dessert is served in heaven?
Angel food cake.

**What does the ocean wear
on its head at night?**
A white cap.

What did one tennis shoe say to the other?
You're sneaky.

What's longer than forever?
Fivever.

What did one smurf say to the other?
Are you okay? You look a little blue.

What do you call a car that is worried?
A nervous wreck.

What do trees eat for breakfast?
Oak-meal.

**What does an apple say
when its fruit is taken?**
Hey, stop picking on me!

What do you call a ball wearing glasses?
An eyeball.

What did one iPod say to the other?
Help me, I'm syncing!

**What did the egg say after it
said something funny?**
I'm just yolking.

What did God say to the first man when he breathed life into him?
Up and Adam!

What do you give a sick lemon?
Lemon-aid.

What book of the Bible do math teachers love best?
Numbers.

What is a director's favorite meal?
Tuna cast-a-role.

What did they award the man who invented the door knocker?
The No-bell Prize.

What kind of vegetable was not welcome on Noah's ark?
A leek.

Where do boats go when they are sick?
To the dock.

Where is a plant's favorite place to rest?
A flower bed.

How do you know water is afraid of heights?
It always runs downhill.

What do you call a sad strawberry?
A blueberry.

What is a rock's favorite type of music?
Rock and Roll.

What is the most popular candy bar in space?
A Milky Way.

Why couldn't the pirate play cards?
Because he was always on the deck.

**What do you get when you throw
a lot of books in the ocean?**
A title wave.

Why did the man take his clock to the vet?
Because it had ticks.

Which is faster—heat or cold?
Heat, you can catch a cold.

**Which school supply is king
of the classroom?**
A ruler.

**How did Benjamin Franklin feel
when he discovered electricity?**
Shocked.

How did the rocket lose its job?
It was fired.

What did the tree say to the fallen branch?
You just didn't get the hang of it.

Why is England the wettest country?
Because the queen has reigned there for years.

What is Noah's favorite state?
Arkansas.

What has a bottom at the top?
Your legs.

What do trees do at a baseball game?
They root, root, root for the home team.

Who was the first person hired in the Bible?
Job.

Where do all the uppercase letters live?
In the capital.

What does an umpire say when lightning hits the ground?
Strike!

What is a baker's favorite drink?
Baking soda.

How does an angel answer the phone?
Halo!

What is a lightbulb's favorite song?
This Little Light of Mine.

What kind of fruit lives in a barn?
A strawberry.

What did the piece of toast wear to bed?
Peanut butter and jammies.

How did the sun know she was sick?
She wasn't feeling too hot.

When is a theater clumsy?
When the curtain falls.

Why did the banana go to the doctor?
It wasn't peeling very well.

What goes, "Ha ha ha," plop?
Someone laughing their head off.

Why was the car so smelly?
It had too much gas.

What do you call a surgeon with eight arms?
A doc-topus.

What do you get when you mix SpongeBob with Albert Einstein?
SpongeBob Smarty Pants.

What did the talking tree say to the amazed girl?
Be-leaf me, it's true!

Why was the clock in trouble during class?
It tocked too much.

What do astronauts do when they get angry?
Blast off!

What does a nosy pepper do?
It gets jalapeño business.

What is the quickest way to double your money?
Fold it in half.

Want to hear a pizza joke?
Never mind, it's too cheesy.

How does a train eat?
It goes chew-chew!

What do you call a Frisbee that doesn't cost anything?
A freebie.

What driver never gets a ticket?
A screwdriver.

What did the happy triangle say to the mad square?
Shape up!

When is the moon the heaviest?
When it's full.

When is a farmer mean?
When he pulls on the ears of corn.

What is God's favorite dessert?
A Sunday.

What did the egg say when it was all right?
I'm yolk-ay!

What state is always in poor health?
Illinois.

What was Boaz like before he got married?
Ruth-less.

What is a drummer's favorite vegetable?
Beets.

How do you make seven an even number?
Take the S out.

What is the loudest sport?
Racquetball.

Why did the shoe take a piece of candy when its mother wasn't looking?
Because it was a sneaker.

Why was the nose sad?
Because it was getting picked on.

What state makes you sneeze?
Mass-*achoo*-setts.

What do you call a wacky baker?
A dough nut.

How did the cereal say goodbye?
Cheerio!

Where do books sleep?
Under their covers.

What did the tooth say when another tooth wouldn't share?
You are rotten!

What kind of nut loves board games?
A chess-nut.

What did the salad say before dinner?
Lettuce pray.

What do you call candy that giggles?
Laughy Taffy.

What did one marble say to the other?
You are marble-ous.

Why can't bad actors catch fish?
They always forget their lines.

What did the digital clock say to its mother?
Look, Mom, no hands!

**What did one bullfighter say
to the other bullfighter?**
What's the matador?

**What day of the week do
potatoes fear most?**
Fry-day.

**What did one elevator say
to the other elevator?**
I think I'm coming down with something.

What do you get when the sun goes surfing?
A heat wave.

What has wheels and a trunk but no engine?
An elephant on roller blades.

Why did the tooth run away?
Because it was loose.

What kind of phone never rings?
A saxophone.

**What did the hot dog say
when it lost the race?**
I just couldn't ketchup.

What is a foot's favorite month?
Oc-toe-ber.

Why didn't they play cards on the ark?
Because Noah was standing on the deck.

How does an egg run?
It scrambles.

**Why did the boy bring logs
into his bedroom?**
He wanted to have a lumber party.

What did the apple tree say to the farmer?
Stop pickin' on me!

What did one flag say to the other flag?
Nothing. It just waved.

Why don't you tell secrets in the corn patch?
There are too many ears.

What did one cherry say to the other cherry?
This is the pits!

Why did the cucumber call 9-1-1?
Because it was in a pickle.

Which book of the Bible is a tree most afraid of?
Acts.

What is a boxer's favorite drink?
Fruit punch.

How do we know that a lot of people in the Bible used fertilizer?
Because they always said, "Lettuce spray." (Let us pray).

What did the needle say to the thread?
Sew, what do you want to do?

What's the best way to study the Bible?
You Luke into it.

Why did the boy have his girlfriend put in jail?
She stole his heart.

**How did the telephone
propose to his girlfriend?**
He gave her a ring.

Why did the boy put candy under his pillow?
Because he wanted sweet dreams.

What did one egg say to the other egg?
Let's get crackin'!

At what time of day was Adam created?
A little before Eve.

**What time is it when you have
to go to the dentist?**
Tooth-hurty.

Where is the first math homework problem mentioned in the Bible?
When God told Adam and Eve to go forth and multiply.

What did the Lego pirate say when he lost his leg?
Where'd my Lego?

What did the farmer say when he opened his barn and his tractor was gone?
Where's my tractor?

What looks just like one half loaf of bread?
The other half!

When does a policeman smell?
When he's on doody.

Where do smart hot dogs go?
To the honor roll.

What do you call a fairy that hasn't had a bath in a while?
Stinkerbell.

What did the beach say when the tide came in?
Long time, no sea.

What is God's favorite ship?
Wor-ship.

How does the moon get clean?
It takes a meteor shower.

Why couldn't the flower ride a bike?
It had lost its petals.

How does a train sneeze?
Ah-choo-choo!

How do you make a cream puff?
Take it jogging.

How long did Cain hate his brother?
As long as he was Abel.

What is a top's favorite food?
Spin-ach.

What is a potato's least favorite day?
Fry-day.

What has a bed but never sleeps?
A river.

Where does a boat go when it's sick?
To the dock.

What did the apple say to the orange?
We make a good pear.

When was meat first mentioned in the Bible?
When Noah took Ham into the ark.

Why did the football coach go to the bank?
To get his quarterback.

**What asks no questions but
must be answered?**
The doorbell.

**What did the mommy car and the
daddy car call their baby-boy car?**
Carson.

**What kind of garden does a
robot like to plant?**
A BOTanical garden.

What has 8 legs, 9 eyes, and 20 hands?
I don't know, but it's crawling up your leg!

Which way did the computer programmer go?
He went dataway.

What do you call a torn piece of paper?
Tear-rible.

What do you call a book about a car?
An autobiography.

How does Moses make his coffee?
Hebrews it.

What did one hand say to the other?
You're so-fist-icated.

What did the doctor say to the invisible man?
I don't see anything wrong with you.

What do you call a train loaded with toffee?
A chew-chew train.

Where is the first tennis match mentioned in the Bible?
When Joseph served in Pharaoh's court.

What did the hamburger name its daughter?
Patty.

How do you have a successful solar-system party?
You planet!

What type of food is the easiest to eat?
A piece of cake.

What disease can authors get?
Authoritis.

What do you call a fake noodle?
An impasta.

Where do athletes go to get new uniforms?
New Jersey.

Why does DNA have no fashion sense?
It always wears the same old genes.

How did the bubblegum cross the road?
It got a ride on the chicken's foot.

What do you call a very polite cop?
A please officer.

Why do opera singers make good sailors?
They can handle the high Cs.

What do you call a dish that didn't get to dinner on time?
A late plate.

How do you get a baby to fall asleep in outer space?
You rocket.

Who was the greatest female businessperson in the Bible?
Pharaoh's daughter. She went down to the bank of the Nile and drew out a little prophet.

Why did the man stop to rest on his way to the computer store?
Because it was a hard drive.

What gets wetter the more it dries?
A towel.

What keeps jazz musicians on Earth?
Groovity.

What is a lumberjack's favorite month?
Sep-TIMBER!

Which word becomes shorter when you add two letters to it?
Short.

What does a computer do when it feels hot?
It opens Windows.

Why did the smart phone need glasses?
Because it lost all of its contacts.

What do astronauts do when they're sorry?
They Apollo-gize.

Why couldn't the sesame seed leave the casino?
Because he was on a roll.

Why didn't Noah go fishing?
He only had two worms.

How do you keep people from stealing your bagel?
You put lox on it.

What do you have if you're holding five apples in one hand and seven in the other?
Big hands.

What kind of bow can never be tied?
A rainbow.

Where will you find a swimmer who can't believe he's drowning?
In de-Nile.

Which nut sneezes a lot?
A cashew.

What has 1,000 legs but can't walk?
2,500 pairs of pants.

Why does the baseball fan bake cakes?
Because he likes to watch the batter.

What part of a tree scares cats?
The bark.

How do you cure a headache in a nail salon?
With a head-icure.

Why did the cookie go to the doctor?
Because he felt crumby.

**Why couldn't the music
teacher open his door?**
Because his keys were on the piano.

What has a head and a tail but no body?
A coin.

What is a volcano's favorite food?
Magma-roni and cheese.

Did Eve ever have a date with Adam?
No, just an apple.

Why was the fire hydrant not working?
Because it was dehydrated.

Why was the oatmeal sad?
No raisin.

Did Delaware a New Jersey?
I don't know but Alaska.

What's black and white and read all over?
A newspaper.

Why does the Statue of Liberty stand in New York harbor?
Because it can't sit down.

How do you make holy water?
Get regular water and boil the devil out of it.

Why couldn't Jonah trust the ocean?
Because he knew there was something fishy about it.

How many feet are in a yard?
That depends on how many people are standing in the yard.

What room has no walls?
A mushroom.

What type of cheese is made backwards?
Edam.

3

Animal Jokes

**What is it called when a cat
wins a dog show?**
A cat-has-trophy.

How does a mouse feel after a shower?
Squeaky clean.

What kind of dog plays football?
A golden retriever.

Why didn't the bull cross the road?
He was a cow-ard.

**What does a bat take to its
first day of school?**
A bat-pack.

What does a calf use to do its homework?
A cow-culator.

**What do you get when you cross
Godzilla and a parrot?**
I don't know, but if he asks for a cracker, give it
to him!

**What do you get when you cross
a cat with an elephant?**
A flat cat.

Why did the grasshopper go to the doctor?
Because he was jumpy.

Why did the bee get married?
Because she loved her honey.

Why do bees have sticky hair?
They use honey combs.

What did the spider do on the computer?
Made a website.

What goes snap, crackle, squeak?
Mice Krispies.

**What kind of animal should you
never play cards with?**
A cheetah.

What do you call a bear with no teeth?
A gummy bear.

What dog can jump higher than a building?
Any dog—buildings can't jump.

Why do fish swim in salt water?

Because pepper makes them sneeze.

What has eight legs and walks on webs?
Four ducks.

How do you paint a rabbit purple?
With purple hare spray.

**What's black and white and
makes a lot of noise?**
A zebra playing drums.

**What do you get when you cross
a chicken and a Chihuahua?**
Pooched eggs.

What animal needs to wear a wig?
A bald eagle.

What's the best way to catch a fish?
Have someone throw it to you.

Where do mice park their boats?
At the hickory dickory dock.

Where did the sheep go on vacation?
The Baaaa-hamas.

What does a cat say when someone steps on its tail?
Me-OW!

What is as big as an elephant but weighs nothing?
It's shadow.

What did the dog say to the flea?
Stop bugging me.

How do you know an elephant has been in your refrigerator?
By the footprints in the butter.

What do you call a dog that likes baths?
A shampoodle.

Where do fish keep their money?
In a river bank.

**What do you call an elephant
that wears perfume?**
A smell-ephant.

**What kind of music do frogs
like to dance to?**
Hip Hop.

Why does a rhino have so many wrinkles?
Because he's hard to iron.

Which bird is always out of breath?
A puffin.

What color do cats like?
Purrrrrrple.

Where do cows get their medicine?
From the farmacy.

What do you call a sleeping bull?
A bulldozer.

Why did the little bird go to the hospital?
To get tweet-ment.

What do you get from a pampered cow?
Spoiled milk.

What is a shark's favorite game to play?
Swallow the leader.

What do cats do before they go to bed?
Prrrrray.

What do you call
a flying skunk?

A smelli-copter.

**What did the buffalo say to his kid
when he dropped him off at school?**
Bison.

**What do you get when you cross
a porcupine and a turtle?**
A slowpoke.

**What do you get when you cross
a potato with an elephant?**
Mashed potatoes.

Why are horses such lousy dancers?
They have two left feet.

**What do you get when you cross
a parrot and a centipede?**
A walkie-talkie.

**What did the duck say when
he bought lipstick?**
Put it on my bill.

**What is gray, has four legs,
a tail, and a trunk?**
A mouse on vacation.

Why did the monkey fall out of the tree?
Because it was dead.

**What do you call a porcupine
that doesn't move?**
A cactus.

What did the horse say when its food ran away?
Hay.

What do you call a grizzly bear caught in the rain?
A drizzly bear.

What do you call a dog that creates books?
A pup-lisher.

What do you call a flying ape?
A hot-air baboon.

Why can't a leopard ever win at hide and seek?
Because it is always spotted.

What do you call a really jumpy dog?
A kanga-roof.

What do you do when you are surrounded by lions, tigers, and cheetahs?
Get off the carousel.

What bird is good to have at every meal?
A swallow.

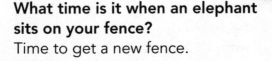

Why did the cow cross the road?

To get to the udder side.

What time is it when an elephant sits on your fence?
Time to get a new fence.

What is a goose's favorite food to eat at a baseball game?
A honk dog.

**What do you get when you cross
a mouse with a squid?**
An eektopus.

Why did the chicken cross the playground?
To get to the other slide.

What do cows say in space?
Mooooo-n.

What do you use to groom a rabbit?
A hare brush.

Where does a bull keep his business papers?
In his beefcase.

**Why don't cats ever need to
go to the eye doctor?**
Because they have purrfect vision.

What do you call a baby ocelot?
An oce-little.

Why did the leopard wear a striped shirt?
So she wouldn't be spotted.

What part of a turkey is musical?
The drumstick.

Why are cats so good at video games?
Because they have nine lives.

Why couldn't the pony sing?
Because he's a little hoarse.

What color socks do bears wear?
They don't wear socks, they have bear feet.

Why did the cat get 100 percent on its test?
It was purrfect.

**What do you get when you cross
a computer with an elephant?**
Lots of memory.

**What's black and white, black
and white, black and white?**
A panda bear rolling down a hill.

Why did the bee go to the doctor?
Because she had hives.

What is the biggest ant in the world?
An eleph-ant.

**What do you get if you cross a
grizzly bear and a harp?**
A bear-faced lyre.

Why are frogs so happy?
Because they eat what bugs them.

Why did the kid throw the butter out the window?
To see the butter fly.

What do you call bears with no ears?
B.

Why didn't the teddy bear eat his lunch?
Because he was stuffed.

What do you call it when it rains chickens and ducks?
Fowl weather.

Why are fish bad at basketball?
Because they're afraid of the net.

Why do seagulls fly over the sea?
Because if they flew over the bay they would be called bagels.

What is a bird's favorite time?
5 o'flock.

Where do milk shakes come from?
Nervous cows.

What do you call a pig that knows karate?
A pork chop.

**Where does a peacock go
when it loses its tail?**
A re-tail store.

**How much money
does a skunk have?**

One scent.

**What kind of bird can carry
the most weight?**
A crane.

**What did one mosquito say
to the other mosquito?**
Want to get a bite with me?

What do polar bears eat for lunch?
Ice berg-ers.

Why was the baby ant confused?
Because all of his uncles were ants.

**What do you get when you cross
an antelope and a caribou?**
A cantaloupe.

**What do you get when you cross
a sheep and a honey bee?**
Bah-humbug.

**What do you get when you cross
a parrot with a shark?**
A bird that will talk your ear off.

**What steps do you take if a tiger
is running towards you?**
Big ones.

What type of dinosaur does things quickly?
Pronto-saurus.

What is black and white and red all over?
A panda bear with a sunburn.

**What did one cow detective
say to the other?**
This case is 'udderly' moo-sterious.

**What do you call someone who put her
right hand in the mouth of a lion?**
Lefty.

What do you do with a blue whale?

Try to cheer it up.

Why can't you shock cows?
They've herd it all.

Why didn't the butterfly go to the dance?
Because it was a moth ball.

What did one frog say to the other?
Time's sure fun when you're having flies.

Why was the mother firefly unhappy?
Because her children weren't that bright.

How do you plan a space party?
You planet early.

Why didn't the boy believe the tiger?
He thought it was a lion.

What's a duck's favorite meal?
Soup and quackers.

**What is black and white and
eats like a horse?**
A zebra.

When is it bad luck to see a black cat?
When you're a mouse.

**What did the farmer call the
cow that had no milk?**
An udder failure.

What do you get when you cross a cocker spaniel, a poodle, and a rooster?
Cockerpoodledoo.

Where do cows go for entertainment?
To the moo-vies.

What kind of horses go out after dark?
Nightmares.

What do you get when you cross a walrus with a bee?
A wallaby.

What's white, furry, and shaped like a tooth?
A molar bear.

What do you get when you cross an octopus and a cow?
An animal that can milk itself.

What happened to the lost cattle?
Nobody's herd.

Why do bears have fur coats?
Because they look silly wearing jackets.

**What do you get if you cross
a teddy bear with a pig?**
A teddy boar.

Why couldn't the skunk play baseball?
Because he always threw foul balls.

Which bug never does its chores?
A lazybug.

Where do polar bears vote?
The North Pole.

Which side of a cheetah has the most spots?
The outside.

Why is a horse like a wedding?
They both need a groom.

What do you call it when a dinosaur crashes his car?
A tyrannosaurus wrecks.

What do farmer birds say while they are harvesting?
Twheat. Too-eat.

What do you get if you cross a kangaroo and a snake?
A jump rope.

How do bears keep their den cool in summer?
They use bear conditioning.

How do bees get to school?
By school buzz.

What kind of animal is very naughty?
A bad-ger.

Why did the spider cross the computer screen?

To get to the other side of the web.

What do you get when you cross a turtle with a porcupine?
A slowpoke.

Why do ducks have flat feet?
To stamp out forest fires.

Why do elephants have flat feet?
To stamp out flaming ducks.

**What time is it when ten tigers
are chasing after you?**
Ten after one.

What is smarter than a talking bird?
A spelling bee.

**What does a snail say when he's
riding on a turtle's back?**
Weeeeeee.

Where do sheep get their wool cut?
At the baa-baa shop.

What do you call a deer with no eye?
No ideer.

What did one shark say to the other while eating a clownfish?
"This tastes funny."

What was T-rex's favorite number?
Eight.

Where do squirrels go before kindergarten?
Tree school.

How does a lion like his meat?
Roar.

How do you get a rhinoceros to stop charging?
Take away his credit card.

What do you call an elephant in a phone booth?
Stuck.

How many tickles does it take to make a squid laugh?
Ten-tickles.

What do snakes study in school?
Hisss-tory.

Why should you watch out when it's raining cats and dogs?
Because you might step in a poodle.

Why do giraffes have long necks?
Because their feet are smelly.

What kind of vehicles do bees drive?

Hummers.

Why wouldn't the shrimp share his treasure?
Because he was a little shellfish.

What do you call a snail on a ship?
A snailor.

**What do you call a sheep
covered in chocolate?**
A chocolate baaaaaar.

**What bird steals from the rich
to give to the poor?**
Robin Hood.

**What did the mother bee
say to the baby bee?**
"Behive yourself."

**Why did the two boa
constrictors get married?**
Because they had a crush on each other.

What do you call a fish with no eyes?
Fsh.

Where do salmon keep their money?
In a riverbank.

Why did the dog go to court?
Because he got a barking ticket.

Why did the bubblegum cross the road?
Because it was stuck to the chicken's foot.

What is an alligator's favorite drink?
Gator-ade.

Why can't you find a good animal doctor?
Animals have a hard time getting into medical school.

How do you catch a squirrel?
Climb up a tree and act like a nut.

Why did the salamander feel lonely?
Because he was newt to the area.

What do you get if a chicken walks across the road, rolls in mud, and crosses back again?
A dirty double crosser.

What is a frog's favorite warm drink?
Hot croako.

What lion never roars?
A dandelion.

What has 12 legs, 6 eyes, 3 tails, and can't see?
Three blind mice.

What's big and gray with horns?
An elephant marching band.

Why do birds fly south?
Because it's too far to walk.

What do cows do on January 1?
They celebrate the "moo" year.

What do you call a really big ant?
A gi-ant.

What goes dot-dot-croak, dot-dash-croak?
Morse Toad.

What is a llama's favorite drink?
Llama-nade.

Where would a dog park his car?
In a barking lot or a grrrage.

Why do you need a license for a dog but not for a cat?

Cats can't drive.

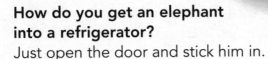

How do you get an elephant into a refrigerator?
Just open the door and stick him in.

How do you put a giraffe into a refrigerator?
First you have to take the elephant out, then you can put the giraffe in.

If all of the animals had a meeting, which one would be missing?
The giraffe, because he's still in the fridge.

Where is a rabbit's favorite place to eat?
IHOP.

What did the orangutan call his wife?
His prime-mate.

What is a horse's favorite state?
Neighbraska.

Why did the crab go to prison?
Because he kept pinching things.

Which dog can tell time?
A watchdog.

What do ducks watch on TV?
Duckumentaries.

Which birds really stick together?
Vel-crows.

Where do orcas hear music?
Orca-stras.

**What do you get when you cross
a fly, a car, and a dog?**
A flying carpet.

**What do you get when you cross
an elephant with a witch?**
I don't know, but she will need a very large
broom!

**What do you get when you cross
a Border collie and a daisy?**
Cauliflower.

Where do rabbits go when they are sick?
To the hops-ital.

Why do bees hum?
Because they don't know the words.

What do you call a thieving alligator?
A crookodile.

What do you name an elephant hiding in a pile of leaves?
Russell.

Where do you get frogs' eggs?
At the spawn shop.

What snakes are found on cars?
Windshield vipers.

What happened to the cat that swallowed a ball of wool?
She had mittens.

When you catch your dog eating a dictionary, what should you do?

Take the words right out of its mouth.

How do oysters call their friends?
On shell phones.

What has four legs and goes "Oom, Oom"?
A cow walking backwards.

**What is worse than a giraffe
with a sore throat?**
A centipede with sore feet.

What do you call a snake in a hard hat?
A boa constructor.

Why didn't the dog eat the homework?
It was too tough for him.

**What do you call a crow that
is too afraid to fly?**
A scared-crow.

Why are fish so smart?
Because they live in schools.

What do you call a cow that won't give milk?
A milk dud.

What fish only swims at night?
A starfish.

Why didn't the chicken cross the road?
Because there was a KFC on the other side.

Where do dogs never shop?
Flea markets.

Why are rabbits so lucky?
They have four rabbit's feet?

What does a robot frog say?
Rib-bot.

**What did the duck do after
he read all these jokes?**
He quacked up.

**What do you call a cold dog
sitting on a bunny?**
A chili dog on a bun.

What mouse was a Roman emperor?
Julius Cheeser.

**Why couldn't the mama octopus
tell her kids apart?**
They were i-tentacle twins.

**Why did the elephant make
a good reporter?**
It had a nose for news.

What do fish do when they lose games of chess?
They whale.

What do you get when you cross a praying mantis with a termite?
A bug that says grace before it eats your house.

What's the difference between a coyote and a flea?
One howls on the prairie, and the other prowls on the hairy.

What piece of equipment do fish use in the army?
A fish tank.

What should you do when you find a jaguar asleep on your bed?
Sleep on the sofa.

What do you call a rabbit with fleas?
Bugs bunny.

Where do crabs wash their clothes?
In tide pools.

How do porcupines kiss?
Very carefully.

What kind of fish chews bubble gum?
A blow-fish.

What do monkeys wear when they cook?

Ape-rons.

Why couldn't the koala take part in the Olympics?
It didn't koala-fy.

Why did the fish go to the library?
To find some bookworms.

Why is a leopard bad at hiding?
Because it's always spotted.

What parts do rabbits sing in the choir?
Hare-mony.

What school did the cat attend?
Kitty-garten.

What animals are on legal documents?
Seals.

What did one owl say to the other owl?
Happy Owl-ween!

Why was the cat afraid of a tree?
It barked.

What do you call a bruise on a T-Rex?
A dino-sore.

How do you stop a bad pig?
Put it in ham-cuffs.

What is the opposite of a hot dog?
A chili dog.

What kind of sickness does a horse get?
Hay fever.

When do you know a cat is joking?
When it's kitten around.

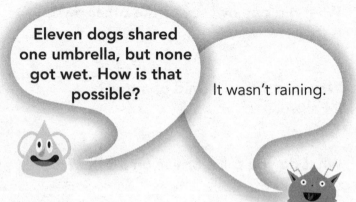

Eleven dogs shared one umbrella, but none got wet. How is that possible?

It wasn't raining.

What do you call a fly without wings?
A walk.

What happened when the owl lost its voice?
It didn't give a hoot.

How do you make a goldfish old?
Take away the g.

What do you call nervous insects?
Jitterbugs.

How do snakes end a fight?
They hiss and make up.

What do you call a horse's story?
A pony tale.

What do you call a kiss from a cow?
A moo-ch.

What do animals in the zoo like to eat?
Zoo-chini.

Why do hummingbirds hum?
Because they don't know the words.

Why didn't the rooster want to fly?
Because he was too chicken.

How do fish sleep underwater?
They snore-kle.

**How many skunks does it take
to stink up a house?**
A phew.

**What's gray and squeaky and
hangs around in caves?**
Stalagmice.

Why did the flies go to France?
They wanted to be French flies.

What do you call a cow with two legs?
Lean meat.

Why does an elephant have a trunk?
Because it would look silly with a glove
compartment.

**What do you call two spiders
who just got married?**
Newlywebs.

**What is the difference between
an elephant and a flea?**
An elephant can have fleas but a flea can't
have elephants.

How do two snails fight?
They slug it out.

What kind of math do birds like?
Owlgebra.

Why did the dog cross the road twice?
It was trying to fetch a boomerang.

What's worse than raining cats and dogs?
Hailing taxis.

What do you call a crying camel?
A humpback wail.

Why did the turkey cross the road?
To prove he wasn't chicken.

How do you keep an elephant in suspense?
I'll tell you tomorrow.

What kind of bench does a stinkbug sit on?
A pew.

Where do horses live?
In the neigh-borhood.

How do you keep a skunk from smelling?
Pinch its nose.

What do you give a sick pig?
Oink-ment.

What do camels use to hide themselves?
Camelflauge.

**What do chicken families do
on Saturday afternoons?**
They go on peck-nics.

**What do you get when you cross
an elephant with a kangaroo?**
Big holes all over Australia.

**What do you call
a cute bulldog?**

An
adora-bulldog.

What do you call a lizard that sings?
A rap-tile.

**How do you tell the difference
between a dog and a tree?**
By the bark.

Why did the squirrel cross the road?
It was nuts.

What's orange and sounds like a parrot?
A carrot.

What is a snake's favorite subject?
Sss-cience.

What instrument do fish play?
The bass guitar.

Why do dogs run in circles?
Because it's hard to run in squares.

Why did the dinosaur cross the road?
Because chickens weren't alive yet.

How does a penguin build its house?
Igloos it together.

How do you catch a unique rabbit?
Unique up on it.

How do you catch a tame rabbit?
Tame way, unique up on it.

Why are snakes hard to fool?
They have no legs to pull.

What do you call an owl with a deep voice?
A growl.

What do whales eat?
Fish and ships.

What do you call a goldfish detective?
A fin-vestigator.

Why did the farmer name his pig Ink?
Because it kept running out of the pen.

What did the boy cat say to the girl cat?

You are very purrrr-ty.

Which animal complains the most?
A whine-oceros.

Which fish can perform operations?
A sturgeon.

What do you call a dinosaur that never gives up?
A try and try-ceratops.

If fruit comes from a fruit tree, where does turkey come from?
A poul-tree.

Why was the dog chasing his tail?
He was trying to make ends meet.

What key won't open any door?
A monkey.

What do you call a bee that never brags?
A humble bee.

What do you call a blind dinosaur?
A Do-you-think-he-saur-us.

Where do tough chickens come from?
Hard-boiled eggs.

What do fish take to stay healthy?
Vitamin sea.

When does a horse talk?
Whinny wants to.

**What do you get when you cross
a dog with a telephone?**
A golden receiver.

**What do angry rodents send
each other for Christmas?**
Cross-mouse cards.

What did the sardine call the submarine?
A can of people.

What do you call a show full of lions?
The mane event.

Why do male deer need braces?
Because they have buck teeth.

**What do you call a bee
having a bad hair day?**
A Frisbee.

What part of a fish weighs the most?
Its scales.

What is a frog's favorite year?
Leap year.

Where do birds invest their money?
In the stork market.

Why did the snowman call his dog "Frost"?
Because Frost bites.

What does a dog eat for breakfast?
Woofles.

What did the lamb say when it was tired?
I'm a little sheepy.

What do you get from an Alaskan cow?
Ice cream.

What kind of mouse does not eat, drink, or walk?
A computer mouse.

Why do dragons sleep during the day?
So they can fight knights.

What happened when two silkworms got into a race?
It ended in a tie.

What is the strongest creature in the sea?
A mussel.

Why did the man buy an elephant instead of a car?
It had a bigger trunk.

What happens to a frog's car when it breaks down?
It gets toad away.

What do you call a
dinosaur that does
not take a bath?

A Stink-o-saurus.

What does a hen do when it sees a fox?
It chickens out.

What does a frog say when it hurts its knee?
"Rubbit!"

What did one bee say to the other?
"It's none of your bzzzness."

**Why did the horse chew
with his mouth open?**
Because he had bad stable manners.

What did the boy bird say to the girl bird?
You're my tweet-heart.

What do you call a great dog detective?
Sherlock Bones.

What do you call an alligator in a vest?
An investigator.

**What musical instrument is
found in the bathroom?**
A tuba toothpaste.

How do you make a tissue dance?
You put a little boogie in it.

**What do you get when you
cross a ghost and a cat?**
A scaredy cat!

What do birds do at the playground?
Ride the tweeter-totter.

What did the owl say when it won the race?
HOO-ray!

Which flower talks the most?
Tulips, of course, because they have two lips!

**What do you get when you cross
a fish and drumsticks?**
Fish sticks.

**What do you get when you cross
a tiger and a blizzard?**
Frostbite!

**What do you get when you cross
a fish with an elephant?**
Swimming trunks.

What do you call a dancing sheep?
A baaaa-llerina.

What do you get when you cross a cow and a lawnmower?
A lawn-moo-er.

What time do ducks wake up?
At the quack of dawn.

What do you get when you cross a cow with a trampoline?
A milk shake!

What do you get when you cross a cat with a fish?

Catfish.

**What do you get when you
cross a frog with a rabbit?**
A bunny ribbit.

**What do you get when you cross
a fridge and a stereo?**
Cool music!

**What do you get when you
cross a lemon and a cat?**
A sourpuss.

What do you call a race car that can't race?
A car.

Why did the man ride the bull?
Because it was too heavy to carry.

**Why did the boy tiptoe in front
of the medicine cabinet?**
He didn't want to wake the sleeping pills.

What do you call cows that are laying down?
Ground beef.

Why did the fastest cat in school get suspended?
'Cuz he was a cheetah.

Why do chicken coops have 2 doors?
If they had 4 doors they would be a chicken sedan.

How do you communicate with a fish?
You drop it a line.

What did the man say to the horse when he walked into the room?
"Why the long face?"

Why did Mozart get rid of his chickens?
They kept saying, "Bach, Bach."

What did the frog order at the burger place?
A hoppy meal and fries.

Knock, knock.
Who's there?
Possum.
Possum who?
Possum food, please. I'm hungry.

Knock, knock.
Who's there?
Rhino.
Rhino who?
Rhino every knock-knock joke there is!

Knock, knock.
Who's there?
Honeybee.
Honeybee who?
Honeybee a dear and open the door.

Knock, knock.
Who's there?
Alpaca.
Alpaca who?
Alpaca the trunk, you pack-a the suitcase.

Knock, knock.
Who's there?
A herd.
A herd who?
A herd you were home, so I came over.

Knock, knock.
Who's there?
Gorilla.
Gorilla who?
Gorilla me a steak, I'm hungry!

Knock, knock.
Who's there?
Cowsgo.
Cowsgo who?
No, they don't. Cowsgo moo!

Knock, knock.
Who's there?
Beaver.
Beaver who?
Beaver-y quiet and no one will hear us!

Knock, knock.
Who's there?
Toucan.
Toucan who?
Toucan play that game!

Knock, knock.
Who's there?
Wood ant.
Wood ant who?
Don't be afraid. I wood ant hurt a fly!

Knock, knock.
Who's there?
Bat.
Bat who?
Bat you'll never guess!

Knock, knock.
Who's there?
Kanga.
Kanga who?
No, kanga roo!

Knock, knock.
Who's there?
Howl.
Howl who?
Howl you know if you don't open the door?

Knock, knock.
Who's there?
Giraffe.
Giraffe who?
Giraffe anything to eat?

Knock, knock.
Who's there?
Aurora.
Aurora who?
Aurora just came from a polar bear.

Knock, knock.
Who's there?
Meow.
Meow who?
Take meow to the ball game!

Knock, knock.
Who's there?
Owls.
Owls who?
That's right, owls whooooooooo!

Knock, knock.
Who's there?
Lion.
Lion who?
Lion on your doorstep, open up!

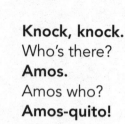

Knock, knock.
Who's there?
Amos.
Amos who?
Amos-quito!

Knock, knock.
Who's there?
Anudder.
Anudder who?
Anudder mosquito!

Knock, knock.
Who's there?
Goat.
Goat who?
Goat to the door and find out!

Knock, knock.
Who's there?
Crab.
Crab who?
Crab me a snack, please.

Knock, knock.
Who's there?
Interrupting cow.
Interrupting c—
Mooooo!

Knock, knock.
Who's there?
Cook.
Cook who?
Stop making bird noises and open the door!

Knock, knock.
Who's there?
Who.
Who who?
Are you an owl?

Knock, knock.
Who's there?
Beehive.
Beehive who?
Beehive yourself!

Knock, knock.
Who's there?
Iguana.
Iguana who?
Iguana tell you another knock-knock joke!

Knock, knock.
Who's there?
Hee-haw.
Hee-haw who?
Are you a donkey or an owl?

4

Holiday/
Seasonal
Jokes

What did one volcano say to the other?
I lava you.

Why did the boy have his girlfriend put in jail?
She stole his heart.

Why did the boy put candy under his pillow?
Because he wanted sweet dreams.

What did the octopus say to his girlfriend when he proposed?
Can I have your hand, hand, hand, hand, hand, hand, hand, hand in marriage?

How did the telephone propose to his girlfriend?
He gave her a ring.

Why was the Easter bunny so upset?
He was having a bad hare day.

**What season is it when you
are on a trampoline?**
Spring time.

Knock, knock.
Who's there?
Sherwood.
Sherwood who?
Sherwood like to be your Valentine!

Knock, knock.
Who's there?
Value.
Value who?
Value be my Valentine?

How does the Easter bunny stay in shape?
Lots of eggsercise.

**What kind of beans do not
grow in a garden?**
Jelly beans.

What happened when the Easter bunny met the rabbit of his dreams?
They lived hoppily ever after!

How can you tell which rabbits are the oldest?
Look for the gray hares.

How do you know carrots are good for your eyes?
Have you ever seen a rabbit with glasses?

Knock, knock.
Who's there?
Esther.
Esther who?
The Esther bunny.

What do you call a rabbit who tells jokes?
A funny bunny.

Knock, knock.
Who's there?
Candy.
Candy who?
Candy Easter bunny carry all those treats in one basket?

What did summer say to winter?
Help. I'm going to fall.

What did Polly the parrot want for the 4th of July?
A fire cracker.

Where was the Declaration of Independence signed?
At the bottom.

What did the flag say to the pole?
Nothing, it just waved.

Why were the first Americans like ants?
They lived in colonies.

What's red, white, black, and blue?
Uncle Sam falling down the stairs.

Why did the skeleton cross the road?
To get to the body shop.

Why didn't the mummy have any friends?
Because he was wrapped up in himself.

What do ghosts eat on Halloween?
Ghoulash.

What position does a ghost play in soccer?
Ghoulie.

What do you do when 50 zombies surround your house?
Hope it's Halloween.

What kind of road has the most ghosts haunting it?
A dead end.

What do ghosts eat for supper?
Spooketti.

Why didn't the skeleton want to go to school?
His heart wasn't in it.

Why didn't the skeleton cross the road?
He didn't have any guts.

What do you call a fat pumpkin?
A plumpkin.

What monster plays tricks on Halloween?
Prank-enstein.

Why are ghosts bad liars?
Because you can see right through them.

What room is useless for a ghost?
The living room.

**What do you call a skeleton
who won't work?**
Lazy bones.

How do you make a skeleton laugh?
Tickle her funny bone.

**Why did the vampire get thrown
out of the haunted house?**
Because he was a pain in the neck.

What do monsters put on their bagels?
Scream cheese.

What do witches put on their hair?
Scare spray.

What does a ghost wear in the rain?
Boooooots.

What is a vampire's favorite fruit?
A neck-tarine.

What's a ghost's favorite fruit?
Boo-berries.

What is a witch's favorite subject in school?
Spelling.

Why do ghosts carry tissues?
Because they have BOOOOgers.

Why didn't the skeleton go to the ball?
Because he had no body to go with.

What is the best way to speak to a monster?
From a long way away.

Why is Superman's costume so tight?
Because he wears a size S.

Why couldn't Dracula's wife get to sleep?
Because of his coffin.

What is a ghost's favorite position in soccer?
Ghoul keeper.

What does a skeleton say before dinner?
Bone appetit!

When is it bad luck to be followed by a black cat?
When you're a mouse.

Who did Frankenstein take to the dance?
His "ghoul" friend!

What kind of dessert does a ghost like?
I scream!

What kind of pants do ghosts wear?
Boo-Jeans.

Why do ghosts make good cheerleaders?
Because they have a lot of spirit.

What kind of music do mummies listen to?
Rap.

What did one ghost say to the other ghost?
Do you believe in humans?

What do vampires take when they are sick?
Coffin drops!

Why are ghosts so bad at lying?
Because you can see right through them.

**What do you get when you cross
a duck with a vampire?**
Count Quackula!

**Where do ghosts
buy their food?**
At the ghost-ery store!

Why did the scarecrow win the Nobel Prize?
Because he was out standing in his field.

**Why should you never leave a turkey
alone with Thanksgiving dinner?**
Because he will gobble, gobble it up.

**What's the sleepiest thing at
Thanksgiving dinner?**
The nap-kins.

**Which side of the turkey has
the most feathers?**
The outside.

What do math teachers do on Thanksgiving?
Count their blessings.

**What do you get when you cross
a turkey with a banjo?**
A turkey that can pluck itself.

Why can't you take a turkey to church?
They use fowl language.

What kind of music did the Pilgrims like?
Plymouth Rock.

Why do turkeys gobble?
Because they never learned their table manners.

What keeps an igloo warm?
Ice-olation.

What rains at the North Pole?
Reindeer.

What breakfast cereal does Frosty the Snowman eat?
Snowflakes.

Where do snowmen go to dance?
A snowball.

Lots of Jokes for Kids

Q: What do you get when you cross a parrot and a centipede?

A: A walkie-talkie!

Q: What kind of light did Noah install on the ark?

A: Floodlights

Introducing a collection of jokes that's hilarious, clean, and kid-friendly and includes everything from knock-knock jokes, to Q&A jokes, tongue twisters, and a whole lot more. *Lots of Jokes for Kids* is certain to have every kid you know laughing out loud, snorting riotously, and generally gasping for air.

Available in stores and online!

ZONDER**kidz**™

Lots of Knock-Knock Jokes for Kids

Whee Winn

Knock, knock.
Who's there?
Woo.
Woo who?
Don't get so excited, it's just a joke!

Knock, knock.
Who's there?
Anita.
Anita who?
Anita borrow a pencil.

New from Zonderkidz, here's a collection of knock-knock jokes that is both hilarious and wholesome. *Lots of Knock-Knock Jokes for Kids* is sure to send every kid you know to his knees in a breath-stealing, side-splitting, uncontrollable fit of giggles. It's that funny. And with more than 350 jokes, the laughs are sure to never quit.

This collection provides fun for the whole family and includes bonus Q& A jokes and riddles too!

Available in stores and online!